Duende de Burque

THE ALBUQUERQUE POET LAUREATE SERIES

Co-published with the City of Albuquerque's
Department of Cultural Services, the Albuquerque
Poet Laureate Series features new and selected work
by the city's Poet Laureate at the conclusion of their
two-year term. Newly appointed poets will join
Hakim Bellamy, Jessica Helen Lopez, Manuel González,
Michelle Otero, and Mary Oishi as significant voices in
the community who have been recognized with
the honor of serving as the Poet Laureate and sharing
their craft in the volumes published in the series.

Also available in The Albuquerque Poet Laureate Series:
Bosque: Poems by Michelle Otero

DUENDE DE BURQUE

ALBURQUERQUE POEMS AND MUSINGS

MANUEL GONZÁLEZ

University of New Mexico Press
City of Albuquerque Department of Cultural Services
Albuquerque

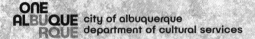

city of albuquerque
department of cultural services

Published in association with the City of Albuquerque
Department of Cultural Services

Library of Congress Cataloging-in-Publication Data
Names: González, Manuel (Poet), author.

Title: Duende de Burque: Albuquerque poems and musings /
    Manuel González.

Other titles: Albuquerque poet laureate series.

Description: Albuquerque: University of New Mexico Press:
    City of Albuquerque Department of Cultural Services, 2021. |
    Series: Albuquerque poet laureate series

Identifiers: LCCN 2020040359 (print) | LCCN 2020040360 (e-book) |
    ISBN 9780826362674 (paperback) | ISBN 9780826362681 (e-book).

Subjects: LCGFT: Poetry.

Classification: LCC PS3607.O56229 D84 2021 (print) |
    LCC PS3607.O56229 (e-book) | DDC 811.6—dc23

LC record available at https://lccn.loc.gov/2020040359

LC e-book record available at https://lccn.loc.gov/2020040360

COVER ILLUSTRATION
Cover photo, *Camino Sábado*, and author photo
by Joel Wigelsworth | joelwigelsworth.com

DESIGNED BY
Mindy Basinger Hill

COMPOSED IN
Minion Pro and Adhesive Nr. Seven

This book is dedicated to Albuquerque, New Mexico. The Sandia mountains. The Rio Grande Bosque. This book is dedicated to our community. Thank you for allowing me to represent you for two years. This book is dedicated to my *familia*, *sangre* or not. It was your support and encouragement that made me the poet I am today. This book is dedicated to the ancestors, the spirits, and the orishas. The Gods that gave birth to the gods that made the world. *Metaki Oyasin*. All my relations. Thank you for helping me shift my consciousness to the left.

I knew

I shoulda taken

that left turn

at Albuquerque.

BUGS BUNNY

CONTENTS

Duende de Burque

For me personally, writing began as a private and personal thing that I kept a secret. As a boy I was always afraid that someone would make fun of me for writing poetry, so I kept it to myself. As I got older I began to share my writing with my friends, who quickly asked me to write poems to the girls they liked in hopes of getting a date. It didn't always work, but it was a reason to write. As I got older I got hip-hop. I was the beatboxer, and my friends and I would cipher all night long, but for me at the time it was like hip-hop was cotton candy. It tasted good and it was fun, but it didn't have the vitamins I needed to survive. I didn't find what I was looking for until I went to a poetry slam.

A poetry slam is a competition where each poet recites a poem they wrote themselves. Every poem is given a score from zero to ten. Zero is a poem that should have never been written, should have been left home. Ten is a poem that causes simultaneous orgasm in a ten-mile radius. I had never experienced someone get on a stage and allow themselves to be emotionally vulnerable and lyrically proficient at the same time.

I started going to the slam, and I started to lose. I would get on stage, and my paper would shake. I pulled my hat down low and hid behind my paper to do what I had to do to get through the poem. But I didn't give up. I revised, rewrote, and memorized my poetry. Eventually I started to win. Winning led to me being able to compete at a national level with world-renowned poets.

I came home on fire with inspiration. Then, during a performance at a reading at a local coffee shop, a teacher approached me and asked me to come into her class and recite my poetry. When I got into the high school there were students who were like me, awkward and full of feelings. I recited poetry for them, and I realized that I was the person who got to show them an art form that I love for the first time. I was the one who got to grab them by their hearts and squeeze them until it hurt. Then I gave them a pen and paper and told them to tell the truth in the best way they knew how, and the floodgates would open. Tears and affirmations in every direction. I had found my calling.

First and foremost I use poetry and literacy as a guise to help me get into places to provide a safe place to cry. Through performance poetry I allow myself to demonstrate emotional vulnerability. This, in turn, allows the audience to open themselves up to authentically express themselves. For some people this can be a very cathartic experience. I have found that most of us carry trauma with us. Some of that trauma started before we were even born. This ancestral trauma needs to be exposed to the light and healed. This is the purpose of my work. This is why I do what I do—because I found power in my vulnerability. By exploring and expressing ancestral trauma we get a deeper understanding of ourselves. Looking within and honestly coming to terms with history has the power to heal. That history includes humanity's conquests and failures and our own personal bruises and scars we carry on our spirit. This is how we cry with our ancestors and mourn. This is how we explore our own personal stories and find the strength that comes from shedding the tears and standing with pride after we set our broken bones straight. After we heal together we can then appreciate the wonder, beauty, and magic that is the world all around us all the time.

Over and over again, in class and after class, I was allowed to cry with students who, some for the very first time, would stand up and claim their identity or express their pain. Together we would explore our experience, our hearts, and our spirits. Then we would share this work with each other. But I don't feel like I ever taught anyone anything. All I did was create a space where authentic self-expression was possible and safe.

Sometimes it takes hard work and a fighting spirit to find the necessary healing. That work can be painful and frightening. But, I found, once we begin this journey, the beauty surrounding us at all times becomes more real. The pain we carry can be a burden we don't notice until we put it down. With that new lightness of spirit comes an appreciation of the sacred. We gain sensitivity to beauty and the inherent goodness within us all.

Authentic self-expression can heal. In life we find ourselves carrying the scars and bruises on our hearts from our past experiences, and the wounds on our souls that were put there before we were even born. We call this ancestral trauma. In order to heal from this pain we carry we have to look inward, and through sincere self-expression we can begin to mend and reconcile our past. That artistic expression isn't always pretty. In fact, sometimes it's full of pain and self-loathing. We sometimes need to find ourselves in a puddle of tears, sweat, and snot. To be real means to expose our shadows to the light. To be sincere means to unashamedly share our shame. Because we all have these injuries of the spirit, the art we create when we heal can be the inspiration the next person needs to begin the journey of healing themselves.

That was the road that led me to become an Albuquerque Poet Laureate.

At the time I really had no idea what it meant to be a Poet Laureate. I was encouraged to apply for the position by close friends, but I never really thought that I was going to win. This title changed my artistic life forever. It legitimized me as an artist. It made people take me and my art seriously. But it also put me in awkward situations and uncomfortable places. I found that I became a representative of Albuquerque. I had the opportunity to travel to places and show people our best—our pride and our culture. But sometimes I was the only "token" brown person in a room, or I was asked to write things that made me evaluate my artistic integrity, and I had to figure out how to balance pleasing paying patrons and at the same time writing with poetic sincerity.

This collection consists mostly of poems that were written during my laureateship and the stories behind them.

First of all, those of us from Albuquerque don't always say *Albuquerque*.
Sometimes we say *Burque*. Burque has a collection of cultures and
people that can't be found anywhere else. Her magic can shift our spirit
to the left. When I became Poet Laureate I knew that I had to represent
Burque in all her beauty. I had to show pride in where I come from. I
feel this first poem encompasses what I feel about Albuquerque. We
are the two-step, the jingle dress, and the *ranchero* dances. We are
all these things simultaneously, and we push past any stereotypes or
misconceptions that people might have about this *tierra* that we have
such a strong connection to.

Summertime heat creates
mirages off the asphalt,
playing tricks on our eyes.
Burque and her secrets
are whispered on the wind
when we listen.

Paletas and sticky smiles
on the faces of *mocosos*
running free without a care for the heat.

The elders know where to find escape
from the hot Zia sun.

The river finds her
home in the bosque,
where we can find solace,
solitude,
and silence
in the middle of a bustling
metropolis.

Burque,
where the thirst of
the *tierra*
is quenched by a
late-afternoon
monsoon,
sun shining through the raindrops
like diamonds.
Precious gems of our memories,
the smell of rain,
flashbacks of puddle jumping.

We celebrate the rain in the desert
like a long-lost friend
returning home.
The streets shine
new and clean
after the flood recedes,
but our parents still
tell the children of
La Llorona
to keep us safe
and away from the deadly
ditches,
arroyos, and acequias that carry
our dreams to irrigate
the milpas in the south valley,
growing the same
corn, beans, and squash.
The three sisters
that were introduced to our ancestors
long ago.
The acequias
carry dreams to quench the thirst
and feed us until our *panza llena*
and our *corazón* is *contento*.

While dragonflies dance
in the amber light of
sunset,
Burque,
so full of history
and culture,
inviting,
welcoming
with pride,

orgullo.

As our skies
as big as our imaginations
hold clouds like floating cathedrals
or carry hot-air balloons
on a crisp morning,
listening to KABQ
while we clean house,
two-stepping with a broom
to Tiny Morrie, Al Hurricane,
or Manny and the Casanovas—
New Mexico Music!
Born and bred
like calabacitas
with corn and green chile
or homemade tortillas.
Alburquerque,
where we honor traditions and history,
sage smoke,
and Chimayó red chile.

Fishing at Tingley Beach
early in the morning
before the ducks wake up.
Burque is who we were.
It's who we are.
It's the legacy we pass on to our children.
Like cruising Central,
Old Route 66,
on a Sunday afternoon
in a 1963 Chevy,
original and clean!
playing oldies,
those oldies that remind us of how far we've come.
Cruising all the way to South Valley gardens
growing community
underneath our Zia sun,
blazing in the sky.

We celebrate each other's
food
music
dance
heartbeat
drumbeat
sacred blessings from the creator.

We are flamenco
and Danza Azteca,
Jingle dress
and two-step,
breakdance
and *rancheras*.
Our heartbeat is the rhythm
we live our lives to.
Our connection
to this land,
this mountain,
this sky!
Our collective sweat
and tears in our eyes.
Memories we share
of river water
and cottonwood trees.
A symphony of *chicharras*.
That hypnotizing drone
is the late-summer song
that our daydreams dance to.
In harmony we hear the crickets
take over the night.

Our singing
with *gritos* that cry out to the sky!
When the sun sets behind the west mesa,
and the Sandias ripen
for that brief fleeting moment
before it gets dark,

our pink mountains' majesty
holds us in her arms.
Another night in the Duke city,
and our *jitos* and *jitas*
are safe and sleeping.
The *viejitas* say their prayers
and light their candles,
and another Albuquerque summer is laid to rest
to become memories and stories,
the stories we all share
as Burquenos!

In New Mexico we have our own music. It sounds like green chile with a rockabilly guitar. It's the South Valley of Burque played with saxophones. The music sounds like *santuario* sand, a good matanza, and the loneliest teardrops dripped into a shot of tequila. This is the music I grew up with. Every Saturday morning my mother would clean the house blasting Tiny Morrie or Roberto Griego. I still associate the smell of Pine Sol with the sound of *rancheras*. We mark every wedding, funeral, *quinceañera*, birthday party, or any other reason to get together with our *rancheras*, *cumbias*, and boleros. This music helps us perpetuate our culture, keep our families together, and teach us who we are.

Music has been a part of my life for as long as I can remember. My father was the leader of a band called "Manny and the Casanovas." This band was one of the originators of New Mexico Music. I love his music, but it's not exactly what you would think. The sound of his music was not always easy to find in our home. He passed away from pancreatic cancer when I was just eighteen months old. I don't have any real memories of my father, but what I do remember is how much it would hurt my mother to hear his music. Every time his music would come on the local New Mexico station (which at the time was KABQ) my mother would break down and cry. They were really in love, and when he was gone the music was a source of pain. People always wanted to dig out my father's albums whenever they saw us, and I knew then that the fun was over and it was time to sit with my mother while she cried. It got to the point where I didn't want to hear my father's music at all, because I didn't want to see my mother cry. That was my first taste of the power that music has.

Even though I never knew my father, his blood pumps through my heart. I love music. It has helped me figure out who I am and how to feel. I must have some of my father in me, because now I use music to get me through the hardest times of my life, and it also helps me celebrate the best of times. It makes the pain, heartache, and struggle that we go through on a daily basis easier. And it makes the beauty, magic, and joy we share even better.

I'm not a professional musician like my father was. I'm a spoken-word poet and a performance artist. I know the power of self-expression and how emotion can be used to move people in deep, personal ways. I don't play the saxophone like my father, but I did teach myself how to play different instruments from around the world. The instruments I've chosen are instruments that hold a resonance for me, because the sounds that they make vibrate in my soul. I use my instruments to help me meditate and further my spiritual journey.

In my opinion all music is good music, but some music you can just feel. It connects us to our families, our histories, and ourselves. It has to make you feel, or think, or move. It has to leave you with something. Anything.

I was remembering my father's saxophone.
Remembering those days when I was angry at God
For taking him from me.
I only had this brass instrument
As a memory of him.
He died when I was a baby.
Instead of a father I had these levers,
These levers that I manipulated with my fingers,
Blowing into the old cracked reed
That once made music from my father's breath.
But that man has always been a stranger to me.
I would blow into that saxophone,
But without proper guidance and instruction
I could only play sour notes.
I played myself into jail.
Every time I tried to play a tune
All I could play were mistakes.
Stumbling through life,
Blowing with all my might,
But randomly pressing levers,
Waiting for the music to come.

CASANOVA SENIOR

I

His doctor said he couldn't possibly father a child
He was too sick
He could hardly even hold his saxophone
But he was ready to be a father
They tried once before
She didn't have the strength to carry him full-term
This time she was determined
Every day she made fresh tortillas, beans, and chile
To fuel her and her baby
Only the food she made with her own hands would stay down
Gave her the strength to complete the journey
The cancer had already ravaged his body
The chemo had taken his hair
But he was still there
The doctors gave him three months
But he saw his son live for eighteen months
Before he was called home
To meet his maker
Leaving her alone
With a child
And his music

It was the lamp's last night
There wasn't enough oil to keep the flame burning
His fire illuminated the faces and warmed the hearts of all of us
He finished his flickering dance with the wind
The cold, cutting, and cunning wind
Blew hard
But the flame just danced
Longer than he was supposed to
Lighting our lives with his own piece of noonday sun
And when he died he left a little flame smouldering in the heart of his
son
And he left his son music so he could learn to dance too
And a little bit of light to illuminate the darkness of grief he left behind

Growing up in New Mexico, my family was very devoutly Catholic. My parents were very involved in the church. When I was a baby my father was already sick, so the priest came to our house and baptized me in a big bowl with a pitcher of holy water. Later I was an altar boy, and I made my first holy communion. Then, when I was old enough, I started the process of being confirmed. That's when I was old enough to ask questions. I was beginning to read. I read Saint John of the Cross and his dark night of the soul. I read *Paradise Lost* and saw the Bible from a new perspective. Eventually my questions stopped being answered by the Church. I began to study Indigenous philosophies. I devoured everything to do with pre-Columbian Mesoamerican theology. Later I found Carlos Casteneda, and I read every book he wrote. I read books by the women who followed him. That began my journey into shamanism. I also began to study Taoism, and *Be Here Now* by Ram Dass changed my life.

My life has been a search for spirituality. When I was twelve years old I went to a preacher-boy camp with the Baptists. I learned how to give a sermon. Now I use that skill to repeat every sermon I've ever heard at a Santana concert. I believe in the concepts revealed to Carlos Casteneda by Don Juan Matus. No human being is perfect, and we can find flaws in all philosophers, but does that mean that the philosophies have to be thrown away too? I don't know, but these ideas really resonated with me.

I studied Mexica thought and philosophy. *Ometeotl!*

I studied Yoruba, Santeria, and the orishas. *Ashe!*

I'm open to anything that resonates with truth. My spirituality is an amalgam of thought from around the world—ascended masters and bodhisattvas.

What ultimately evolved into my present-day spiritual beliefs started with my nose in a book. Then I moved on to meditation and journeys into the mind. Exploring psychedelics, studying Terrence McKenna, sweating with sundancers, creating my own rituals that I performed alone by the river, and following a disciplined meditation regime are what helped me write these poems. I haven't figured anything out yet, but this is a reflection of the journey I've been on.

HEART BEAT

As the wind blows
It fills my soul
With the voices of my ancestors
Telling me to forgive the transgressors
It's like meditation when the thought ceases
It's like Coltrane cutting his soul to pieces
The vibration increases with each beat of the drum
Connecting me to the one
OM
As my words become spirals
I spin into the infinite vastness of my consciousness
Eliminating my fears
While I'm thinking in spheres

Where am I?
Here
What time is it?
Now

How to be like Einstein
Transcending space and time
Getting closer to the divine
Opening my eyes
Letting me realize the skies
I can see that the rhythm of the earth
Is connected to the heart

Heart beat

The rhythm of the universe
Begins with your pulse
Connecting me to
The one
The I
The three
And for the first time I can actually see
It's like remembering forever
Before and after
We are all bastards of humanity
And all divine children of infinity
But don't walk toward insanity
Because most of humanity is still lost
Searching for ourselves
While afraid of who we are
When we're all just made
Of the same substance as stars

SUM TOTAL OF ME

Understanding the limits of my psyche
Might be the first step to finding limitlessness
Finding my boundaries and breaking them
Learning about journeys and taking them
Shaking my cities to their foundations
Then remaking them
Like the tower of Babble
It's important that you see what I'm saying
And realize that all sight
Doesn't come from the eyes
But the sight that stays on the prize
Is the vision
Of this mission
I'm still looking for truth
And for freedom
But now I'm meeting orishas
And learning how to feed them
I'm trying to decipher the code
Of my dreams
With mystic tools
And ancient rules
And elemental spirits to teach me lessons
On how to make confessions
And libations
To the guardians of the four directions

East
South
West
North
The heavens and the earth
And all points in between
Pointing me to Huitzalopochitli's hummingbird
The smoking mirrors of
Tezcatlipoca

Mixed with the memories of
Mi Vida Loca
And the incantations from
Mi Boca
My first holy communion with
Wind
Fire
Water
Earth
The trumpet calls
I can hear it
It's time to dare
To will
To know
To be silent
The nagual is all around me
Sounds be grounding
Rhythms resounding
Reversing and rebounding
Reverberating with the vibrations
Of realizations yet to come
The sum total
Of me

And I thank the ancestors of humanity
And the spirits of possibility
For assisting me
On my quest for liberty
Through my words
And my actions
I try to show respect
Now the only thing left
Is to take that breath

Mouth movements
Manipulating monoliths
Making my mind masticate
Massive mathematics
Like the golden ratio
And the tree of life
Light lightening bolting its way to the top
Faster than sight
Looking for the heights of humanity
Drowning in complacency
Trying to save enough energy to
Open our heart and truly see

See?

When the clock strikes now

(at the sound of the tone the time will be . . . now)

OM

Creating sacred spaces
Allowing my tongue to twist
As he
Double
He licks her spiral spaces
And all of God's good graces
And the aces are sleeveless

As my mind breaks out
Running in four directions
Remembering heaven
While still respecting
The spirit of the Earth
And for what it's worth
Spiral staircases
Speak in spiritual spheres
And ancient ancestral warriors
Wage war on wayward fears
As the lucid dreamer looks left
And finds the dreaming
And he sweats as he sings
To grandfather stones
Looking for the meaning

EMPRESS OF ETERNITY

An ekphrastic poem inspired
by "Compass and Key" by Carlos Quinto

I

Repeated mantras
Unlock consciousness
The Empress sits
On her throne.
Earth mother, cloaked in awareness,
Knows
The truth behind the veil
As the holy angel of death
Prostrates himself before
Her diamond-studded shoes
The enchantress
High priestess of the moon
Purest and most exalted
Spiritual form of Isis
Incomparably dazzling
Guardian of the key
Guadalupe Tonantzin

Repeated mantras
Unlock consciousness
With iris dilated
We see eternity
Dancing
Ring around the rosie
Concentric circles
Completing cycles
Time
Space
The compass IS the key!
To unlock and enter buddha's center
Life and death
Symmetry and balance
Powerful vulnerability
Creating perfect circles
The sacred idea behind the form
Flower of life
Seeing deep inside
To the center of
Formlessness

Repeated mantras
Unlock consciousness
The empress of the wilderness
Steps on the compass that
Creates perfection
While Quetzalcoatl coils
Around another egg
Another epoch
Another aeon
From every direction nebulas shine
To help the lotus to open and
Kundalini to climb
Goddess of the green
With her heart chakra
Exposed
Fearless in her vulnerability
Christ is but a seed
And with enough faith will grow into a tree
Sacred geometry
To measure the circumference of reality
Ritual and ceremony
Locks and keys
To unlock blocked chakras
She is grounded in intuition and
Imagination
The inspiration that comes when the
Circle is complete

MANIFESTATION

Forum and formlessness
from my cerebral cortex
these are the words that I manifest
outside time and space
I find a place
where Consciousness exists
and persists
your perception
becomes intention
and reflection
at the moment of Ascension
one mind connection
a Circle was already cast so there's plenty of protection
the ancestors are present and well-fed
traditional rituals mixed with symbols
that fit the individual
are visible
the candles are lit
sitting in the sand from the *santuario*
libations are poured to feed the spirits who whisper wisdom in the Wind
once again It's time to begin
the story of the boy who was afraid of his own Magic
is tragic
there were so many moments of mistakes
he couldn't hear it though because he couldn't find the silence
he didn't believe in his own abilities
to speak to the trees and witness the warrior Spirit of the Wind
he wanted to hear his ancestors but he forgot the Nahuatl
so he searched his dreams for signs and symbols
bringing back rimes and sigils
but he woke up every morning so angry at the world and himself
that the wealth of his dreams was lost to the daymares that he made
for himself
by hiding from his own destiny
he was son of a musician

magician whose magic moved the dance halls of vodka in the sixties
and seventies but his father was a memory made by stories told to boys
whose fathers died when they were babies

the full moon shines her light into my spirit
giving me insight
into my own Darkness
I've become comfortable
with the stale stagnant air I breathe
and like the full moon
I have to face the shadows
and the Darkness

like a deer in the headlights
I know that
everything will be alright if
I
just
don't
move . . .

if I don't move I can't fuck anything else up
and maybe I won't have to face
my mistakes and insecurities

the moon
she has mercy on me
I'm the prodigal poet
returning drunk on my own
stench and shame
afraid to ask for forgiveness
because there's no Redemption
from a life wasted
on smoke and mirrors
the narcissistic high
that comes from the infatuation with
one's own voice
I've become everything I hate
as I get closer to my dreams

my eyes are closed
hoping the monsters under my bed
can't tear through the sheets
while La Luna
looks at me
with love and understanding
she knows
mine is a struggle of substance
while my worries
wax and wane
waiting for the moonlight memories to fade
but I can still smell Destiny on the breeze
and my ancestors wrote
the rhythms on my heart

When I approach a school I ask to be put in the hardest classes. I want to go to the classes full of knuckleheads. I became good at breaking the ice of hardened students. This led me to work with incarcerated youth.

I can be paid to work with the more affluent schools, but I prefer to go where the students actually need me—where there are hurting students who have no outlet, no way to positively work through their negative emotions.

I try to make the classroom a safe, nonjudgmental space. I encourage free speech. But when I'm working with young people who have lived long, hard lives in their few years, I find that they often have an urge to write about sex, drugs, violence, and negativity. I encourage this as a way into a sincere discussion about these topics. But we quickly get to a place where we need to change our way of thinking and find pride within ourselves. So I had to find ways to help gently direct their writing in a different direction.

The first and most effective technique is one I use to work with the hardest cases, who need individual attention. I begin by writing a leading sentence on a piece of paper. I usually use something vague but poetic, something like the color of hate or the sound of anger. Then we pass the paper back and forth. Without speaking, we each write a "metaphorical" response to the previous line. That's where I go in for the emotional center of what we are writing about. This is a safe way for tough kids to authentically express themselves. All I ask is honesty and introspection.

The second technique is useful with all writing levels and styles. I begin by saying that when it's time for me to write, the hardest thing for me to do is begin. Looking at a blank sheet of paper always intimidates me; I have a hard time pulling ideas out of the sky. So I give all the students the same first line so they don't have blank pages. I usually use, "I'm here today to speak the truth," or, "I need to look deep inside myself to see how I feel." Not only do I give the students the first line, but I also give them the first word or phrase for each line, because however we end each line will be the way we begin the next line. The repetition helps spark inspiration. After we emotionally vomit everything onto the page, we can then edit that work into something we can be proud to call poetry.

This is how I helped the hardest of the incarcerated get real and write something powerfully vulnerable. But in order for me to ask them to go there, I had to demonstrate it first. Here are a few examples I use to help young people look inside themselves to find truth.

TRUTH

I'm here today to speak
the truth
The truth is . . .
We all struggle
Struggle makes us stronger
We get strength by not giving in
to our temptations and vices
that just hold us back
Back in the day
I made my mistakes,
but I learned
I learned to speak with my words
instead of my knuckles
that have been bloodied and bruised
battling demons,
demons that know my fears
I know my fears are just an illusion
An illusion in my mind
My mind creates poetry in order to heal
Heal not only myself but those in need of healing
True healing comes from within
Within each and every one of us is power,
the power to change our own
realities and master our destiny.

I'm here today to speak
the truth
The truth is . . .
Shadows run from the light
The light of day expels darkness,
the darkness that exists within us all
All of humanity breathes
Our breath is one of the places to find power
The power to change
Change our lives
Change the world
The world evolves with each trip around the sun
The sun that keeps our daydreams warm
                Dreaming while awake is the best way to find inspiration
The inspiration that can move the
hearts of the wounded
The wounded that need healing
That kind of healing that comes from
within and
within us all is the   power
The power to change the world

So,
                Change the world!

I'm here today to speak the truth
              The truth is the most powerful weapon
My weapon is my mind
               My mind is filled with dreams
Dreams of beauty
             The most beautifullest thing in this world
                  is love
                     Love for our family our people our culture
Culture is the beauty we create
             We create our own realities
Reality is sometimes a hard thing to look at
                          I look into the eyes
            of spirit storms searching for the calm

            The calm is broken by the thunder

          Thunderous heartbreaks and lightning-fast fears
             I fear the sunshine
                    because I've befriended my shadows
My shadows are getting old
I'm too old
already
to hold me down
                like this

I'm here today to speak

                  the truth

The truth is

                                        we all make mistakes

                Those mistakes make us learn

We learn who we are

what we want to be

and what not to do

                Do what you gotta do to survive

                        but make sure you gotta have pride

Be proud to live by your convictions

and be a person of substance

              A person of substance speaks from their hearts

                        and means what they say

What we say is the truth

                The truth is my word

                        My word is all I have in this world

            In this world, there are traps meant to get us off our path

Our path that leads to our destiny

                    our destiny that cannot be avoided

V

I'm here today to speak the truth
The truth is that I sometimes get overwhelmed by life
Life gets heavy and my shoulders get sore from carrying all my worries
Those worries are simply shadows
Imposters
Imposters passing as demons
Demons with power
The power they have was given to them by me
Me,
I sometimes view the world through tear-filled eyes
Eyes that cry because of the pain of emotional scars
Emotional scars that need healing
The healing of the soul
The spirit
The spirit is strong
And will be stronger because of the pain

WALLS UP AND PROTECTED

For all incarcerated children

They come into the room
Skeptical and guarded
We introduce ourselves to each other
To them, this is routine habit
I'm looking for a reason to praise them
Hoping they will open up and talk

After we get to know each other a bit
I get to introduce them to poetry
Poetry is an art form that either they don't know
Or they have bad connotations of
I get to be the first one
To grab their hearts and squeeze
Show them the power of this art form
I've learned to love so much
With life and emotion, I tell stories of pain and heartache
Reality and hope

With each poem, their walls start coming down
And at the perfect moment
When they start vibrating
I give them paper and a pen
And ask them to begin
Then the floodgates open

What they write is raw and real
Viscerally moving stories of mean streets
Broken families and bullshit bravado
Mixed with powerful vulnerability
I get to watch
As they learn to use simile and metaphor
To protect the parts that get exposed
When we express ourselves this way
Forcing them to find their power somewhere
Other than the barrel of a gun
Or their knuckles

First
I had to earn their trust by
Going there
And bringing back tears to show that even a strong man cries
They feel my catharsis and see
That it's okay for us to show our emotions
Be compassionate
Stand up against injustice
I speak directly to the warrior spirit within them
Showing sincerity
And they know it

I give them some gimmicky writing assignment
Involving looking within themselves
And writing about what they see there
They begin to define themselves by telling their stories
Looking for the broken or sore spots in their hearts
And begin to heal
Together we learn that this is how we stop
Making the same mistakes over and over again
This is how we stop making the same mistakes over and over again
Over and over again
This is how we find the lessons that we need to learn
Mirror reflection
Introspection
Poetry
Healing

My journey into poetry brought me to prisons, to children in prisons. I know that authentic self-expression has the power to heal, and our stories hold value. I work with incarcerated children to help them heal their own spirits by writing their stories into poetry. Those stories, when told honestly, without trying to glorify the violence, help put together the shattered hearts and lives of these kids. Even though they are treated like hardened criminals every day, they have the light and life of childhood in their eyes. Sometimes we have to get over the hurdles of toxic masculinity and misogyny to find that hope and light, but it's there. Poetry has taken me all over the world, but I want to be where I'm needed, places where the healing that comes from authentic self-expression is needed. This poem was written at the New Mexico Youth Diagnostic and Detention Center. Kid Prison.

ANCIENT AZTEC ORIGAMI

Dedicated to the boys at YDDC Detention Center

Folding future memories
Into modern codices.
Honoring ancestors by giving old graffiti glyphs new life.
Slicing time
With our tongues like a knife
From the center of the *Quinto Sol.*
Obsidian blade cutting through silence
Making our new language whole.
Huitzilopochtli hummingbird hovers
Over the flower of life, and
Drinks life's nectar, and
Tastes the sweetness of infinite symbology
Breaking up tags into
Graffiti numerology
Counting the signs
Searching for direction
But the subtlety of images
Breaks away from artistic preconceptions.

Allowing imagination to run free.

Manifesting mystic messages
Hoping to see
The next codex
Recording history.

To be burned in the fire.

But like a phoenix from the flames
It's time to give ourselves new names.
Returning to the beginning.
Putting Coyolxauhqui back together.
Trying to remember
The significance of the womb
The magnificence of the moon
And the inevitability of the tomb.

Muerte makes mortality meaningful.

Amazed at the ways the soul plays with the page
Creating symbols of sorrow and rage.
While tattoo teardrops take time to fall.
Permanent pictures of pain
Can't be washed away by the rain
Or incinerated by the flame.
Needing someone to blame
We incarcerate creativity
Keeping kids quiet
Silence their poetry
Hiding their identity

But ancestral knowledge is genetic.
Can't forget it.
It's in our DNA.
These spirialing scrolls hold
Wisdom old.
Tezcatlipoca spoke of smoking mirrors.
Mysteries hidden but
We're making vision clearer.
Sight turned inward to see spirit
Soul can be dark
But there's no reason to fear it.

It's visceral and mystical
Full of magick and messages
To be seen in dreams.
Ollin Mexica
Making a movement
El Movimiento Estudiantil
Ayotzinapa students kidnapped and killed!
Igniting a revolution
Burning down old towers of oppression

Of sins against self
Redefining wealth
Exploring the possibility
Of salvation through self-expression.

Journeying with Mictlantecuhtili
Laughing with our mortality
Knowing there's more to reality
Than what can be seen by the eyes
It's like that life-changing moment
When we first realize
That the heartbeat is the rhythm of the universe.
So we write a verse to express that connection
And make
Time
Rhyme
With
Mind
Seeking the sensation
Of meditation.
Kissing Kundalini
While our chakras are spinning into infinity.
We write our own histories.
Making new creation myths
To birth a new ideology.
The codex was burned
But we already learned
The symbology

Blood and bones
Tears shed alone
Yearning for home
Words written in stone

We honor ceremony and ritual.
Daily devotions become habitual.
The discipline it takes to journey to the other side.
Where we're exposed with nothing to hide
We can take control of our own stories
And begin to heal.
We heal from the wounds that scar the spirit by
Drawing a picture of our pain and
Painting a portrait of what makes us proud
Because when we leave this place
All that will be left will be
That face on the shroud.

During my laureateship I was invited to conduct a workshop on healing through authentic self-expression and connecting to ancestors through digging in our roots at the CULTURE/SHIFT conference. This intercultural, intergenerational gathering brought people from across the country for skill-building, relationship-building, and engaged learning, deepening a movement for cultural democracy. CULTURE/SHIFT 2018 was hosted in partnership with the City of Albuquerque Department of Cultural Services and New Mexico–based arts and social-justice organizations. Together we created, explored, and amplified strategies for cultural healing, resilience, and resistance. It was a national convening of artists, organizers, and allies inciting creativity and social imagination to shape a culture of empathy, equity, and belonging.

During the conference I went from lecture to lecture carrying a notebook with me. The notes I took were a collection of strong "power phrases" that were begging to become a poem. This poem basically wrote itself.

We need to shift consciousness
Artistically shift awareness
Create a new pedagogy
We define the world
Each of us has a unique perspective
Shift the narrative
With powerful vulnerability
We speak truth to power
Armed with our hearts
We create change
By creating connections
With our stories
Our voices
Our ancestors
The vibration of the Uni-Verse
OM

The revolution has begun
The revolution has never stopped spinning
Revolving
Evolving
Encompassing
Including

                      Because
           Ain't nobody free until we're all free!
                              One voice
                              One heart
                              One mind
              Aho Metaki Oyasin

WE ARE ALL ARTISTS!
And as artists we create culture
WE ARE ALL ARTISTS!
Critiquing social structures
WE ARE ALL ARTISTS!
We are the organizers

                                        The leaders
                        The storytellers
                                        The watchers

(observers)

                        The narrator

Shift the narrative

II

What they don't know
What they'll never understand is
Arte es mystico
It must be felt
Can't be explained
Heartbeat rhythms
            In syncopation
With universal truths
One band
            One sound
Until all that is left
Is the resonance

                    We stay grounded in history
                    Standing on the shoulders
                    Of untold stories

                        Voices

                Silenced by the passage of time

                    We are simultaneously
                    Forward-looking
                    And

Historically relevant

Dancing the rain down from the sky
Us
Collectively
Multimedia poetry
Power and prayer
We shift the narrative by
Weaving our unique perspectives
Into public spaces

This is what we mean by community
Cultural sustainability
Intersectional connections
Protection of sacred land
We understand
Systematic environmental racism
The violence of industry
Colonization
Assimilation
But remember . . .
THIS IS TIWA LAND!

III

The sacred circle has been drawn
The eagle and the condor fly together
All signs and symbols are signaling change
The ceremonies and rituals
Have called upon our spirit allies

Ashe

Power

The orishas come to witness
And some ride us like the wind
So we can create art
With intention
THE MOUNTAIN HOLDS POWER
PRAY IN THAT DIRECTION!

Spiritual mercenaries
We nonviolently
Obliterate the patriarchy
Living every day of our lives as ceremony
And our very existence
Is an act of resistance!

We *shift the narrative*
By bringing the medicine that we carry
In our arte
Healing ourselves in the process
Finding forgiveness
Redemption
Breath
Acknowledgment
And release
So we can
Shift the narrative

For me Taos, New Mexico, has always been a magical place where spiritual-
ity, art, and culture come together. When I was young we would go up there
to see real art made by real artists from the Taos Pueblo. It's a place where
santeros search for the piece of wood that calls to them because it wants to
be carved into a saint—a tradition that goes back hundreds of years before
the conquistadores. Taos still has places where you can follow the foot-
steps of Kit Carson or Billy the Kid. I've noticed that there are also a lot of
ashrams, temples, and churches in Taos. Taos is the first place anyone ever
built homes out of reusable, biodegradable materials. The hippies started
that stuff in the sixties in actual communes, and they called their houses
earth ships. See, it's a magical place.

During my laureateship I was asked by the Albuquerque Museum of Art
to attend an art opening and write a poem in response to that art opening.
It was an exposition of the collection amassed by Mabel Dodge Luhan.

Mabel Dodge Luhan was an heiress from Buffalo, New York. She has
been credited with showing and bringing the artistic world to Taos. She is
the reason Taos is such an artistic mecca today.

So I found myself walking through the museum, admiring the beautiful
artwork on the walls. The work I saw there was amazing. I was at home.
I saw my culture on display at its best for the world to see. I was standing
taller, proud of where I came from. As I looked closer I started to notice
paintings of certain sacred ceremonies that are not meant for the public.
Ceremonies that we don't even speak of because of how seriously we take
them. I saw the paintings of the land that I love so much in such beautiful
detail, but I noticed that the artists all had Dutch and German names. That's
when I started to realize that Mabel's legacy is the appropriation of my
culture as a New Mexican. I saw how they chose sacred moments to paint
and how they took those images around the world but gave nothing back to
the people they painted. I started to feel sick because I really wanted to do a
good job and write a poem that was authentic to my experience, but I also
wanted the museum to work with me again. I was conflicted. I couldn't just
write some pretty pastoral piece about the paintings. I had to call out the
appropriation. This poem is the most gentle compromise I could come to
and still hold on to my artistic integrity.

THE DUALITY OF TAOS

For Mabel Dodge Luhan

                              I remember the gorge
Gorgeous in its grandeur
                                        Reminding me of my insignificance
                    Taos
Full of secrets and duality
                    Beauty
                    Creativity
                    And poverty
              Colors and Cultures
          Contacts and connections
The intersection of
Pueblo, Hispano, and Anglo
The cultural catalyst
Beating heart of the world
A place where the blood of penitentes
                              Flows like the Rio Grande onto canvas
The heartbreaking beauty of sunsets that
                    Color the palette with warm hues of stolen dreams
Themes of struggle
Scenes of sacred images
With movement and action
                    The reaction to Taos
The town that hums
And the drums can still be heard

                                        Beating loud

Drawing in
          Artists and poets
Warriors and wisemen
                    Shamans
                    And
                                        Charlatans
Billy the Kid, Kit Carson, and
                    The Matachines

                              Coral and turquoise concha belts for the tourists
The tourists intent on taking part of us home with them
                                                        Just one taste

One tear
One breathless gasp
Holding history in their grasp
And taking it home to hold in their hearts
                                                    Until it bears artistic fruit
                          Strange fruit
                              Full of sacred images and secret imaginings

Our skin and sweat
Ceremony and dance
Our skies and scenery
The beauty
Of the Taos valley
                          And it's duality
                                                    Exploitation of reality
Artistic interpretations of
                                                    Our light and color
Now
                          Priceless artifacts
                                        To hang on museum walls

The Prado in Albuquerque was an art exhibition in downtown Albuquerque, and all the Poets Laureate were invited to write a response to one of the pieces in the show. The exhibition featured pieces from the Spanish royal family's collection in the Prado Museum. The Prado Museum opened in 1819 and is Spain's main national art museum.

So there I was walking in front of the convention center in downtown Albuquerque, looking at all of these paintings that were considered to be masterpieces by the greatest artists, but all I could see were images of our colonizer. Whether it was the celebration of the conquest and conquistadores or the iconography of Christianity, it was an art exhibition that celebrated Spain's conquest of this New World. For some of us, that is a sore subject.

I kept thinking about assimilation, subjugation, and colonization. The phrases that were going through my mind were things like "cultural rape" and "genocidal conquest." I couldn't hand these people a poem in response to these paintings and still remain true to my artistic integrity.

I was dumbfounded and worried until I found a painting of a group of men standing in line on the shore of the ocean, blindfolded in front of a firing squad. Antonio Gisbert Pérez, by royal decree on January 21, 1886, was commissioned to paint a large historical painting exemplifying the defense of freedom for future generations. The work intended to convey that the defense of freedom was the execution by firing squad of General Torrijos and his closest unconditional followers, who had been the outstanding protagonists of the constitutional regime during the Liberal Triennium that was quashed by Ferdinand VII in 1823. The more I studied this piece the more I became inspired. I saw resistance and struggle against subjugation. This is the poem that came from it.

THE EXECUTION OF
TORRIJOS ANTONIO GISBERT

There are ideas worth dying for
There comes a time when the injustice becomes too much
Our shoulders cannot bear the weight
Silence in the face of oppression becomes betrayal
Cowards backed by armies
Condemn to death our ideals
Kneeling on the shores of the ocean
Talking directly to God
At this last moment
While we are blinded by the church
The government
The powers that be
A sense of dread and foreboding
Freedom is not defeated today
Making martyrs of these men
Ignites a fire in the hearts of
Little future revolutionaries
That watch the last rites
Being read to their heroes
Before they become a memory
Used to change the world
End the oppression of the people
Companeros preparing to die
While the ocean laps hungrily
At the shore
Thirsty for blood
Fourteen men
Awaiting a meeting with their maker
For a cause
Fighting for righteousness
For freedom
With eyes blindfolded
So the soldiers won't have to look at
The last stare of a man dying

Because of his beliefs
They might find their own reflection
A connection to
These men who stand
In stoicism
Hands bound loosely
As they awaited their destiny
To become a memory
That scars the very souls of those left behind
Families without a father
Our leaders were taken from us in a hail of bullets
Incarcerated
Executed
But there is an existence worse than death
To watch the dignity of a people stripped
Children ripped from everything they know
To stand by and allow the machinations of the machine
Chew up the most vulnerable
And spit them out broken
Mangled
And powerless
This is too much to bear
So it is better to become a martyr
To die so that our children can live
Without the brutality of subjugation
The abuse and tyranny
We cannot allow those in power
To exploit the weak and powerless
So it is better to face our own mortality
With courage and conviction
To become a symbol of freedom and humanity
To die on the shores of our outrage
So that our principals will live on
So that the authoritarianism and oppression
Will die with us

I was the third Poet Laureate in Albuquerque. The inaugural Poet Laure-
ate was Hakim Bellamy, and the second Poet Laureate was Jessica Helen
Lopez. I have stood in awe of these amazing artists. They have moved
my soul and inspired me to be a better artist. We were approached to
create a collaborative piece and perform that piece together as a group.

In our poetry community we very often write with each other. We
create "group poems." Sometimes these group poems are a scripting of
one person's poem to become a multivoiced piece. Sometimes they are
a braiding of already written work with similar themes. "Vamos Juntos"
was a completely original collaborative poem that Jessica, Hakim, and I
wrote together then scripted to show all our strengths.

The problem with these group pieces is that, like this piece, we put
our hearts into them. We write, script, and rehearse these poems only to
perform them once or for one summer, but after that the poem dies. If it
was never recorded, it never sees the light of day again. It's such a shame
that we lose this amazing art after the performances. "Vamos Juntos"
was performed only once.

a collaborative poem by
Manuel González, Albuquerque Poet Laureate Emeritus, 2016–2018
Jessica Helen Lopez, Albuquerque Poet Laureate Emeritus, 2014–2016
Hakim Bellamy, Inaugural Albuquerque Poet Laureate, 2012–2014

En lak'ech

            You are my other self
            Nosotros somos tu

Together we create culture

            collaboration

                       and cooperation

Become the manifestation

            We need each other

the way the blossom needs the water,
the stalk and stem need the root,
the way the root is cradled within the good dirt,
moistened earth and foundation

Nature's way of saying collaboration

            is our favorite lifeboat

Nature's way of saying collaboration

            is our highest self

When it's time to take the task head-on

        The more heads the better

Together,

            we shall overcome

                       Si se puede!

Each voice so quiet when alone

            Can become a crescendo

                Crashing on the shore like a choir

We need each other
The way Desi needed
Luci's red-haired humor and she his

                                    infectious Cubano-lilted drawl

(Lucccccccccyyyyyyyy, I'm Home)

The way Linus needs his blanket

                        The way Don Quijote needs Sancho Panza

The way Scooby needs his snacks

                     The way Abbot always confounded Costello

(Hey Abbbbottttttt!)

Our minds.

                Our hearts.

                                Our hands.

Together

We dance
protected by three volcanoes

                Four if you invite the Sandias

                          to this rug-cutting ceremony
          that is impossible to hold . . . alone.

As we do-si-do this valley

                   and sing in the shadow of the Mountains
        The Rio Grande carries our dreams to the sea

I need you
You need me
We need
each other

The Rio Grande brings us back to each other

                because sometimes a partnership is nothing less than
the push and pull

        of the earth and the moon.

Together we ignite inspiration like

a candle
a brown paper bag
and sand

Like the stone
the petroglyph
and the land

But in New Mexico,

we eat good and well enough to know
that it's mathematically impossible to feast day alone

We are corn beans and squash
We are chile, carne, and tortilla
We are the santuario, the sand, and the pilgrim

We are a whole bunch of things that go together . . .

. . . and it's poetic
. . . like letters

. . . becoming palabras
. . . becoming "I know you"
and "I love you"
and "I need you"
. . . becoming completing each other's sentences
. . . becoming completing

each other.

Like the way the heart of Downtown

needs the beat of creativity
Like the way the economy of ABQ

needs ten thousand jobs!
Like the way the health of our town needs
anchors

We source locally
for growth
of *this* city.

Together

              we build across sectors, stitching our
          stories, our strengths like a great rainbow-hued
                 tapestry.

And it is impossible to spell community without N-M

                                        Without U and I . . .
We are of community, *building* community

                        one kaleidoscopic gleaming glass at a time
Rungs on a ladder working together

                     to reach the everlasting sky.

And in the spirit of giving and gratitude we

                           climb forward

             onward
One star does not a constellation make
                     and with skies as big as ours
       a one-note symphony just won't do

We reach
fingertips to tickle
the tops of clouds

Albuquerque

                       is the other end of a love letter.
To hold on to the most important thing we have

each other.

I feel that a Poet Laureateship is not about the specific poet carrying that title. It's about being an ambassador for poetry. It's about having the privilege of sharing the art form that changed and sometimes saved our lives. Being a Poet Laureate means spreading the gospel of authentic and sincere self-expression to anyone willing to listen. It means we need to encourage others to pick up the pen, look deep inside, and write something real about what they see there. Sometimes we get to witness someone having a cathartic breakthrough in front of our very eyes. We see healing and magic so often that sometimes we take it for granted.

In this last section, I'm sharing my version of a workshop I facilitate because I want you to use it. Sit down, breathe deep, and be real. Then I want you to use it. Use it in classrooms, therapy sessions, creative-writing workshops, or anywhere else healing is needed. It's my emotional variation on a pantoum. Please use it! I've shared so many tears with so many people of all backgrounds, ages, and writing levels with this exercise. It works.

This prompt is my variation of a pantoum.

First, choose an emotion.

Close your eyes and relax. Breathe slowly and deeply. Focus on your breathing. When you know which emotion you need to write about, open your eyes and begin. Each step should be one short and concise sentence. Try to feel your emotion while you write. Be honest.

First Stanza

1. Definition: Define your emotion, but not necessarily using the dictionary definition. Describe how that emotion feels to you. How does it manifest itself? What is your experience of that emotion like? What can you compare it to? "Depression is the days the shadows chase me everywhere I go, and my face never dries from the tears rolling down."

2. Color: Compare your emotion to color. What color resembles your emotion, and what images can you think of that are that same color? "Happiness is yellow like the sunshine on a spring day."

3. Time: Put your emotion in the context of time. How is your perception of time changed by that emotion? Each moment can carve a valley into your sanity as it passes, or maybe when you feel the emotion you find that time goes by unnoticed. "Depression is the acid rain dripping onto my tongue, making each moment taste like passing pain."

4. Sound: Compare your emotion to a sound. What sounds resemble your emotion? What sounds do you hear when you feel your emotion? "Anger is the sound of cars crashing, glass breaking, metal bending."

Second Stanza

2. Color. You have a choice here. You can either repeat your #2 sentence verbatim, or you can write a new sentence where you keep the emotion but change the color or give new images that are the same color.

5. New Sentence. All bets are off. You need to look within yourself and find the true origin of your emotion. Be sincere and write an authentic sentence about your chosen emotion.

4. Sound. You have a choice here. You can either repeat your #4 sentence verbatim, or you can write a new sentence where you keep the emotion but change the sound.

6. New Sentence. All bets are off. You need to look within yourself and find the true origin of your emotion. Be genuine and write a real sentence about your chosen emotion.

Third Stanza
5. Now you can either repeat your #5 sentence verbatim, or you can try to write the same sentiments with different words.

7. New Sentence. Why do you feel this way? What are the triggers that make you feel this emotion? How intense is this feeling? Describe.

6. Now you can either repeat your #6 sentence verbatim, or you can try to write the same sentiments with different words.

8. New Sentence. Describe a tangible object that either reminds you of this emotion, or a tangible object that resembles this emotion.

Fourth Stanza
7. Now you can either repeat your #7 sentence verbatim, or you can try to write the same sentiments with different words.

3. Time. Now you can either repeat your #3 sentence verbatim, or you can try to write the same sentiments with different words.

8. Now you can either repeat your #8 sentence verbatim, or you can try to write the same sentiments with different words.

1. Now you can either repeat your #1 sentence verbatim, or you can try to write the same sentiments with different words. Has your definition of this emotion changed or deepened after taking this journey? How?

Make sure to ground yourself when you're done. Plant your feet firmly on the floor and feel the Earth beneath you.

HEALING

An emotional pantoum
for the protests in the summer of 2020

Stop and breathe deep and slow, do it again
Our blood spills red on the street
Old wounds need to be opened up and cleaned in order to heal properly
Burning and looting, weeping and wailing, gunshots echo in my mind,

Our blood spills red on the street again
Bring down old monuments to hate
Burning and looting, weeping and wailing, gunshots into practitioners of peace
Using tears and breath to battle brutality

Bring down old monuments to hate
Heart beating, we are flesh and bone. All of us here together
Using tears and breath to battle brutality
Our cries for justice can be heard whispered in the wind. The time is now

Heart beating, we are flesh and bone. All of us together.
Old wounds need to be opened up and cleaned in order to heal properly
Our cries for justice can be heard whispered by our ancestors. The time is now.
Stop and breathe. Deep and slow. Do it again